Note from the author:

Dear Parents,

It is striking how helpless a parent can feel in the face of his child. When a person is touched by M.S., the entire family is greatly affected. Each person has their own tremendous perspective. It is important to acknowledge that even the little people in the family have their own big views and concerns regarding the illness. They also have their own needs. How these needs are met is crucial to the empowerment and healing of children.

My experience as a child life specialist has enabled me to see the challenges of families living lives with illness. Growing up with a mother who has Multiple Sclerosis, I have actually felt many of these challenges.

It is my hope and pleasure to share with you a bit of knowledge that may aid in guiding your child through this difficult time. Have faith in your ability as parent, teacher, and friend. You hold the power to light your child's way.

Sincerely,

Kim Harrold

Publication date 2005
ISBN 1-59630-006-X

Library of Congress Cataloging-in-Publication Data

Harrold, Kimberly, 1970-
  Sometimes M.S. is Yucky / Kimberly Harrold ; Illustrated by Eric Whitfield.
      p. cm.
   ISBN 1-59630-006-X (alk. paper)
  1. Multiple sclerosis--Popular works. I. Whitfield, Eric T., 1972- II. Title.

  RC377.H37 2005
  616.8'34--dc22
                                2005031360

𝕾cience & 𝕳umanities 𝕻ress
  PO Box 7151
  Chesterfield, MO 63006
  (636) 394-4950
  sciencehumanitiespress .com

This book is dedicated to Mom.
You are our inspiration. We love you.

--Kim and Eric

Special Thank You to:

The faculty at Utica College who began my foundation of Child Life knowledge that appears in this book.

The staff and families at Children's Hospital at Strong who continued my education both professionally and personally. Many ideas for the therapeutic activities in this book began there.

My mother--who not only taught me about MS--she taught me the importance of courage, love, optimism, and a sense of humor.

Sometimes
MS is Yucky

My Mom is differ-

ent from most

other

Mommies.

Her body can't

work like mine can.

My Mom is sick.

Her sickness has a big name: MULTIPLE

SCLEROSIS.

We call it M.S. because it's easier to say.

Sometimes, I get sick too.

But it's a different kind of sick. I get bet-ter. Mom stays sick be-

cause M.S. doesn't go away.

Sometimes, Mom's arms and legs don't hear

her when she tells them to move.

Mom can't always walk,

so she has a wheelchair.

She gives me rides.

Sometimes, Mom's whole body gets really tired and makes her want to sleep.

When she's tired, she can't play with me.

It makes me feel sad.

It's okay to be sad.

Sometimes,
Mom's eyes
don't always
see
everything that
she looks at.
Sometimes, it's
hard for her to
say words.
Sometimes, she
forgets things.

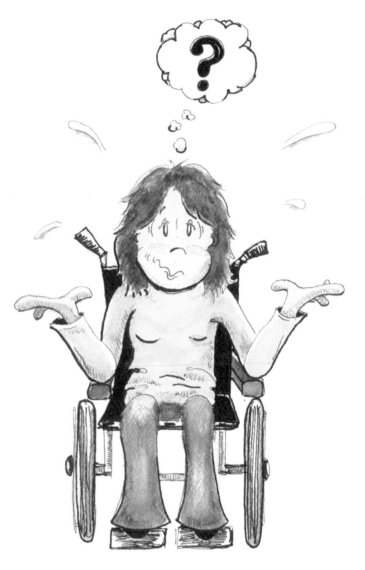

M.S. is hard to understand.

Sometimes, Mom's body hurts.

Sometimes, her hands shake

even though she doesn't want them too.

She drops things. She spills things.

So do I.

But I don't have M.S.

Sometimes, Mom can't write.

She's pretty good at coloring though.

I help her stay in the lines.

Sometimes, Mom takes medicine.

Sometimes, the nurse comes to our house.

Sometimes, she goes to see the doctor.

Some days she feels good.

Some days she feels bad.

Sometimes, the M.S. makes my Mom mad.

She yells.

She's not mad at me.

Sometimes, the M.S. makes my Mom feel

sad.

She cries.

It's not my fault.

Sometimes, I get scared

that Mom will die from M.S.

I talk to her about my scary feelings.

Sometimes, I wonder if I'll catch M.S. too.

Mom tells me I won't get M.S.

because it doesn't have germs.

I can catch a cold,

but I can't catch M.S.

Sometimes, I need to help Mom do things.

Sometimes, I like helping.

Sometimes, I don't.

Sometimes, I feel angry with Mommy

because she is different.

I tell Mom I'm angry.

She hugs me.

I feel better.

Sometimes, we both feel sad at the same time.

We make silly faces at each other.

We laugh.

We feel happy again.

Sometimes, M.S. is yucky.

But........

Always, Mommy loves me very much.

Always, I love her with all my heart.

This helps the yuckiness go away.

Notes to Parents and Caregivers:

Honesty is Still the Best Policy

Be open and honest. When answering questions and offering explanations, being too vague will prompt the child to fill in the blanks with his imagination. A child's imagination can be much more frightening than the truth. It is a parent's natural instinct to want to protect. You can monitor how much you say. There is no need for all the details. Too much information can be overwhelming. The brief, accurate account works best. Take into consideration your child's developmental level. Put your words into kid language. This picture book will give you some ideas of how you might do that. Follow its lead.This book is written for 3-8 year olds. But even a 2 year old can benefit with guidance. Focus on points that she may be drawn to in the book. For example, the emotion on the characters' faces. Or the familiarity of the funny word, M.S.

Normalcy

Keep things as "normal" as possible. Children continue to thrive when kept on a routine. It is fine if a routine needs to be revised due to unpredictable symptoms and/or progression of the Multiple Sclerosis. As long as there are some consistencies that remain in the overall daily routine, it will make a world of difference. A child will feel powerless, frustrated, and unsafe when he does not have control over his immediate world. A regular routine that includes "normal kid" play time can help a child adjust to challenging situations, and also support his natural development.

Do encourage your child to help around the house with special, age-appropriate jobs. This will make him feel like the important part of the family unit that he is. He needs to feel that he can contribute. Just remember not to overwhelm with responsibility. Keep it simple and helpful. A gentle reminder: expressing gratitude and praise for a child's heartfelt attempts can go a long way in building that child's self-esteem.

Transform Foreign Territory into Familiar Ground

Unfamiliar medical situations are enough to make adults cringe. Now do your best to look through the eyes of your child. Your M.S. may find your child witnessing you with medical equipment or personnel.

There are ways to make these scenarios more familiar and less threatening. Explain in simple language what each piece of equipment is used for. You can soften some terminology. For example, if you need to receive an injection or IV start, you can say, "Mommy needs to get a poke. It will give me special medicine to help me feel better.". Ask your doctor or nurse for a syringe and/or IV start (without the needles) that your child can keep at home and play with. Keep this in mind for other pieces of medical equipment as well.

Encourage role-playing. You and your child can play doctor/patient, or you can offer a doll or teddy bear on which to perform procedures. Explain how doctors, nurses, home health aides, physical therapists, etc. help you.

If an occasional hospital stay is necessary, and time permits, visit the hospital ahead of time with your child. Prepare her for the sights, smells, and sounds/voices she might hear. Remember to tell her what you will look like when she comes to see you. This approach will make this potentially traumatic time more of a positive learning experience.

To arrange this type of visit, contact your hospital's Child Life Department and explain the situation. Child life specialists are specifically trained in the field of child development and the impact of medical situations on children. They are prepared to help alleviate the type of emotional distress that could occur, giving hospital tours tailored to the child's perspective.

If there is no Child Life Department, then speak with your doctor or a nurse on the floor where your stay will take place. Greatly encourage-- but do not force your child to visit you in the hospital. Always follow your child's cues. Respect what she is and is not emotionally prepared to face. If she does not want to go, do your best to reassure her that her decision is okay with you and that you still love her just as much. This will help discourage feelings of guilt. In the future, continue to give her the choice. When she is ready, she will let you know.

Symptoms

When teaching about symptoms, keep in mind that young children learn best hands-on. So, put on your best sense of humor and make a game of it. You have your own unique set of M.S. symptoms. Think about what you feel physically while living with this illness. How can you convey some of this to your child in a safe, fun,developmentally appropriate manner? I have included ideas for tremors and speech difficulties. Follow suit and tailor some other activities to fit your situation.What might you do to have your child experience deteriorating eyesight, frustrating limbs, or the need for a wheelchair? What symptoms are pertinent to your situation? Get creative and be playful!

Tremors:

Gently shake your child's hand or arm while he attempts to perform an activity. He could be coloring/writing or trying to place a ball or piece of fruit into a basket. Stand over bathtub or sink. Remember not to leave your child unattended as you do some water play. How easy is it to pour water into a container when your arm is shaking? What types of tasks in his daily routine become difficult? What might he need help with?

Speech difficulties:

Sit down facing each other. Have your child grasp the tip of his tongue with his fingers. Try to talk to each other. Is it difficult to speak? Can it be frustrating?

Feelings

When approaching a child's feelings, perhaps the most precious gift one can give is validation. Reassure her that it is okay and normal to feel sad, angry, frustrated, frightened, guilty, embarrassed, etc. Make it clear that you love her no matter what. Also let her know that nothing to do with the M.S. is her fault. Remember that crying is a natural coping mechanism. It is not a sign of weakness. On the contrary, it is actually necessary at times to maintain your strength. This applies to you, the parent, as well. Do not think that you are a being a bad parent if, on occasion, you cry in front of or with your child. Seeing this human side of you will confirm to your child the fact that it is healthy to feel and express emotions.

Try using a doll, stuffed animal, or puppet. It can be a fun, non-threatening way to encourage a child to share feelings. She might open up more readily to this type of friend, than to you. She could be afraid that her feelings will upset you. Or maybe she is just not ready to share. Do not attempt to force your child to talk about her feelings. Make yourself available in a loving, accepting fashion.

Open the door and extend the invitation. When your child is ready, she will step through. Respect your child's emotional needs and boundaries. Young children are not yet as verbal as older children and adults. They need you to understand this and help them learn how to work through and express feelings in alternative ways.

The following is a list suggesting therapeutic activities that you can facilitate with your child to provide her with a positive outlet for feelings. As you engage her in these activities, remember to let her lead you. Whether or not a discussion is launched, know that she is doing her own healing work.Use the following activities or just simple play sessions to help you gain insight into your little one's heart, as the two of you connect in a special way.

Angry feelings:

- Use a pinwheel to blow angry feelings away. Help child develop a strong, deep, and ultimately relaxing breathing pattern. Have him watch the colors spin, also inducing a relaxing effect. Encourage him to imagine his angry feelings being blown out of his body as the pinwheel sends them far away.
- Hand the child a red or black crayon and a piece of paper. Tell him to show you how angry he is.
- Rip up paper.
- Draw a picture of or write down what is making him angry. When he is finished, suggest that he stomp on it, rip or crumple it and throw in garbage.
- Punch a pillow.
- Throw beanbags at a target. You can make target significant. For example; write the letters, MS, on a piece of paper and hang up.
- Draw, color or paint. Give him his own creative space. Do not dictate what or how

to do it. Allow him to create from his soul--
not from your directions.

•Finger painting, play-dough/clay, and
shaving cream are all excellent outlets.
The child is able to express himself physically and emotionally with these activities.
•Give him some instruments (homemade
work just as well) to play or bang on!

Sad feelings:

- Use bubbles to blow sad feelings away. Have child imagine his sad feelings leaving his body as he blows. These feelings enter the bubbles, are carried away, and disappear when the bubbles pop.
- Blow sad feelings into a balloon. Help child pinch balloon closed with fingers to trap feelings inside. Have child let go of balloon. Watch it fly around the room, as the air comes out. This is symbolic of letting go of feelings.
- Draw, color, or paint. Give him his own creative space. Do not dictate what or how to do it. Allow him to create from his soul-- not from your directions.
- Help him dictate or write a letter to his loved one who has M.S., or to the disease itself.
- Have him do some finger painting. Not only can he express his feelings creatively, the tactile stimulation is soothing and comforting.
- Give him some instruments to play.

At the End of the Day

  If possible, set aside some quality time for you and your child. Review the day's events. You can help her make peace with any lingering anxieties. This way, she can go to bed with a smile on her lips, ready to jump into another day. Maybe read a bedtime story. Definitely think about starting a "Happy Journal". Your child can keep it under her pillow or in another secret spot. Help her think of one happy or funny thing that happened during her day. Or she can think of one thing that she is thankful for. Have her draw a picture or help her write for each entry. If this is difficult for one or both of you, try using a tape recorder to record your entries. You know how funny you sound on tape? This almost guarantees some of your evenings ending with giggle sessions. How you both will treasure this time together. Your child will learn that optimism, and keeping a sense of humor can paint a sometimes bleak world with beautiful colors.

Finally, never forget to set aside time for yourself. What is it that helps you relax? What makes you feel good? Listening to music? Keeping your own "Happy Journal"? Whatever your thing may be... do it! Make sure you have a good support system. Who listens to you? You need to take care of yourself emotionally, as well as physically. The more you nurture your own soul, the better you'll become at nurturing your child's.

Important Note

Have faith in the fact that you know your child best. If you have concerns that your child is having a particularly difficult time dealing with your illness, do not be afraid to seek professional help. If you are not sure where to turn, your doctor or social worker should be able to point you in the right direction.

A book I have found useful is ***How to Help Children Through a Parent's Serious Illness*** by Kathleen McCue and Ron Bonn (St. Martin's Press, 1996)

I would also like to acknowledge that the theory found in the "Parent/Caregiver section stems from combined academic education and professional experience. Supporting theory may be found in the textbook, ***Child Life in Hospitals—Theory and Practice*** by Richard H. Thompson and Gene Stanford (Charles C. Thomas, Publisher, 1981)

About the Author:

The author, Kimberly Whitfield Harrold, was a young child when her mother was diagnosed with Multiple Sclerosis. Her professional background has included working in the fields of child life, therapeutic recreation, and early childhood/ family education. She lives in central New York with her husband and 4 year old daughter.

About the Illustrator:

Kim's brother, Eric Whitfield (or "Icky" as he is still referred to lovingly by his big sister), lives with his wife and baby twins in Central New York.

Both of his parents are established artists. Eric carries on the family tradition and has illustrated a number of children's books.

"Sometimes MS is Yucky" is one example of his passion.

In the words of the illustrator, "I hope you dig it".

Related Books from Science & Humanities Press:

HOW TO TRAVEL—A Guidebook for Persons with a Disability – Fred Rosen (1997) ISBN 1-888725-05-2, 5½ X 8½, 120 pp, $14.95

HOW TO TRAVEL in Canada—A Guidebook for A Visitor with a Disability – Fred Rosen (2000) ISBN 1-888725-26-5, 5½X8¼, 180 pp, $16.95.

AVOIDING Attendants from HELL: A Practical Guide to Finding, Hiring & Keeping Personal Care Attendants 2nd Edn—June Price, (2002), Paper ISBN 1-888725-60-5, 8¼X6½, 200 pp, $18.95

The Job—Eric Whitfield (2001) A story of self-discovery in the context of the death of a grandfather.. A book to read and share in times of change and Grieving. ISBN 1-888725-68-0, 5½ X 8¼, 100 pp, $14.95

Books illustrated by Eric Whitfield

The Gift of the Magic -and other enchanting character-building stories for smart teenage girls who want to grow up to be strong women. Richard Showstack, (2004) 1-888725-64-8 5½ X8¼, 145 pp, $14.95

A Horse Named Peggy-and other enchanting character-building stories for smart teenage boys who want to grow up to be good men. Richard Showstack, (2004) 1-888725-66-4. 5½ X8¼, 145 pp, $14.95

Educators Discount Policy

To encourage use of our books for education, educators can purchase three or more books (mixed titles) on our standard discount schedule for resellers. See **sciencehumanitiespress.com/educator/educator.html** for more detail or call

Science & Humanities Press, PO Box 7151, Chesterfield MO 63006-7151

636-394-4950